The Teen Witches

Tarot

Written by Claire Philip

Illustrated by Luna Valentine

ARCTURUS

ARCTURUS

This edition published in 2023 by Arcturus Publishing Limited
26/27 Bickels Yard, 151–153 Bermondsey Street,
London SE1 3HA

Text adapted from *The Essential Book of Tarot* by Alice Ekrek.

Author: Claire Philip
Illustrator: Luna Valentine
Designer: Rosie Bellwood
Editors: Donna Gregory and Rebecca Razo
Editorial Manager: Joe Harris
Indexer: Lisa Footitt

ISBN: 978-1-3988-2569-7
CH010261NT
Supplier 29, Date 0123, PI 00002501

Printed in China

Contents

The World of Tarot

Introduction

The tarot is a mystical deck of cards that can help you understand what's going on in your life—and make decisions about what to do next. Once you are familiar with the tarot, you can use it to tune in to hidden messages in your subconscious—or gain insight from our vast, mysterious Universe. It is an empowering tool for self-discovery!

All you need is a quiet space, a deck of tarot cards, and some time to reflect on the meaning of the cards you pull during a "reading." This book will show you how to use your deck, decipher the cards, and more.

Imagine that your mind is an iceberg. The conscious (thinking) part is the small section floating above the water. The rest of the iceberg, stretching deep below the surface, is the subconscious. This is where most of your thoughts, experiences, and beliefs are stored. The tarot can be a gentle way to explore this part of your mind, which strongly influences your actions and decision-making.

HISTORY OF THE TAROT

It is believed that people have been using some form of the tarot ever since the 1600s—many of the symbols and pictures on the cards reflect the European medieval and Renaissance periods. There are also clear influences from ancient Egypt, ancient Greece, astrology, and the Kabbalah: a school of thought in Jewish mysticism.

The first set of tarot cards that we know of is from Italy and is called the Visconti-Sforza pack. The second set is known as the Charles VI pack, named after a king of France.

Even though the cards have a long history, they have a timeless quality that speaks to people across all cultures, which is why they are still so popular. After all, the experiences, thoughts, feelings, and emotions that the cards represent apply to us all.

WHAT MAKES UP A TAROT DECK?

A tarot deck is made up of 78 cards, 56 of which are divided into four suits and known as the Minor Arcana. The remaining 22 are picture cards known as the Major Arcana. The Minor Arcana cards correspond to the suits in ordinary playing cards and have a set of court cards—a king, queen, knight, and page. The Major Arcana cards are often numbered 0–21, starting with the Fool at 0 and ending with the World at 21.

Arcana is a Latin word meaning "secret," "mystery," or "mysterious." It refers to the mysteries that the tarot helps us to uncover!

CHOOSING A DECK

There are hundreds of different designs out there, so getting started can be confusing. One of the most common decks is the Rider-Waite-Smith, or Rider-Waite, pack—we refer to this set of cards throughout this book. It's a good place to start because many other decks use it as a template.

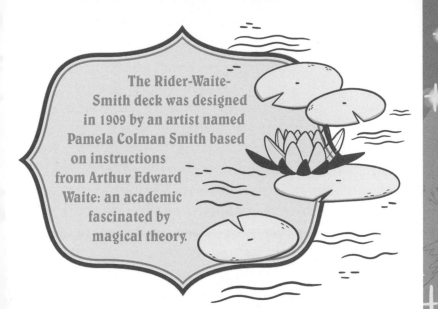

The Rider-Waite-Smith deck was designed in 1909 by an artist named Pamela Colman Smith based on instructions from Arthur Edward Waite: an academic fascinated by magical theory.

Once you have your deck, start learning the meanings of the cards by using this book. When you have a good understanding of their symbolism, you can start figuring out what they mean in relation to your own life. Over time, this will help you develop your intuition (your sense of inner knowing).

CARE OF THE CARDS

Your cards should be stored in a private place, such as a box, when you aren't using them. It's important to form a bond with your cards, so try to avoid allowing other people to handle them.

TAROT CORRESPONDENCES

This table shows how the cards in the Minor Arcana correspond to different qualities, aspects, and elements. During a reading, you can refer to it to build up your knowledge of the cards.

Tarot suit	WANDS	CUPS
Playing card suit	Clubs	Hearts
Element	Fire	Water
Season	Spring	Summer
Timing	Days	Weeks
Qualities	Action, creativity, energy, enterprise, intuition, hope, potential	Love, relationships, happiness, harmony, sensitivity, emotion, contentment

SWORDS	PENTACLES
Spades	Diamonds
Air	Earth
Autumn	Winter
Months	Years
Ideas, communication, conflict, struggle, resolution, change	Money, work, school, talent, reputation, achievement, stability, the living world

COMMON MEANINGS

Knowledge of the following recurring themes can help you during a tarot reading.

- When many cards of the same suit turn up in a reading, it can mean that a particular element or quality is present (see Tarot Correspondences on pages 10–11).
- If there are lots of Major Arcana cards, external influences are likely to determine the outcome of the situation you are asking about. This can mean that the matter is out of your control.
- Mostly Minor Arcana cards can mean that the matter is directly in your hands.
- Aces represent new beginnings, and depending on their position in a spread, they may mean that the answer to a specific question is "yes."

Court Cards

If a court card appears in a reading, it could represent someone in your life that has the character traits associated with that card. It can also represent qualities that you need to develop.

- Kings represent masculine authority figures who embody power, fatherliness, achievement, and responsibility.
- Queens are mature, maternal figures of authority and embody wisdom, confidence, and life-giving qualities.
- Knights represent people who can be rash in their decision-making and who can put themselves first at the expense of others. They also indicate change or movement in a new direction.
- Pages relate to teenagers or young children and represent the potential of youth and dreams. Their qualities need plenty of care if they are to develop; they can also be messengers.

Reversed Cards

When cards are reversed (upside down) in a spread, the meaning is essentially the opposite of the one they have when upright. Some people only use the upright meaning, which is what we use in this book.

TIPS FOR READING THE CARDS

On one level, the tarot is a form of fortune telling, but really, it is more than that. The cards can offer us insights into the forces that are at work in our lives and our innermost selves. Because of this, we should always be humble, compassionate, and sensitive whenever we ask the tarot a question—whether we are alone or with others.

Sometimes the tarot will give us a reading that doesn't make sense. If this happens, take a short break from the cards, and try again later when you are feeling peaceful.

NO SCARY READINGS!

When reading the tarot, always look for the positive. If you pull a card you don't like, remember that the purpose of the cards is to be helpful. The tarot reminds us that we are co-creators of our lives, and that the creative process runs in cycles.

Some of the images on the cards can seem worrying at first, but the deck is always on your side. Pulling the Death card, for example, can mean that it is time to let an outdated part of your personality go, or "die," in the symbolic sense.

The cards can reflect how you are feeling about a situation and provide you with insight. So if you are feeling fear when you pull a card, you may well see an image that reflects that—it doesn't mean there is impending doom. Phew!

PREPARING FOR A READING

Before the cards are laid out, they must be shuffled. As you shuffle, breathe deeply and focus your mind on the question being asked (by yourself or another person). You can either split the deck or fan it out on a table before drawing the number of cards required.

Make sure you place the pulled cards down in the order that you pick them up. Some people like to leave the cards face down and turn each one over as they come to them during the reading—it's up to you!

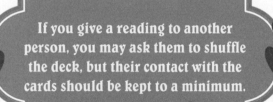

If you give a reading to another person, you may ask them to shuffle the deck, but their contact with the cards should be kept to a minimum.

SELECTING A SIGNIFIER

A card can be chosen to signify yourself or another
person—this card is called a signifier and is usually
the court card (page, knight, queen, king) that best
describes the person. The signifier can be taken out
of the deck and placed in the middle of or next to the
spread to set the tone of the reading—or it can be left
in the deck. (If it is pulled, it can then be understood to
represent the person in the reading or the
person's qualities.)

Your First Tarot Spreads

Tarot Spreads

A single card can be selected from the deck to answer a question or provide insight into an event. Alternatively, one of the following spreads in this section can be used. There are many more ways to lay out the cards, but here are a few of the most popular.

THE THREE-CARD SPREAD

One of the simplest tarot spreads is the three-card spread. The first card is picked and then placed face up. This card represents the past. The second card is taken and placed to the right of the first card—it represents the present. Lastly, the third card is placed on the far right. It represents the future.

Example: Sanu has asked about a friendship that hasn't worked out and is asking the cards to shed some light on the situation.

The past–The Lovers
The present–The Sun
The future–The Hierophant

EXPLANATION

Card 1–The past

The Lovers card represents the experience of having a deep connection with another person. In this past position, it could mean the friendship was very important to both parties, making it difficult for them to move on from it.

Card 2–The present

The Sun in this position suggests that Sanu should focus on herself and her healing at this time. To recover from the ending of her friendship, she should seek joy by following her dreams and working toward her goals.

Card 3–The future

The Hierophant in the future position indicates that the ending of the friendship has led to personal growth for Sanu—and that, in time, she will be able to appreciate the important lessons she has learned.

THE RELATIONSHIP SPREAD

This spread can help you understand your relationship with another person, whether that's your boyfriend, girlfriend, your teacher, family member, or a friend. Since it is a spread for the relationship between two people, make sure you think of the person (not the situation) as you shuffle.

Example: Niamh wishes to know where she stands with her crush, who is acting aloof.

What you think of the other person–The Emperor
What they think of you–Queen of Swords
The strengths of the relationship– The Devil
The obstacles in the relationship–The Star
Where you are right now–The Empress
What influences are likely to come into play–Ace of Cups
The outcome–Two of Swords

EXPLANATION

Card 1–What you think of the other person

The Emperor in this position indicates that Niamh's crush can come across as overbearing—or that she thinks of him as a leader.

Card 2–What they think of you

The Queen of Swords is analytical, strong, and extremely honest. In this position, it could mean that Niamh's crush likes her because of these qualities—or it could mean that their problems are caused by the fact that they are very similar!

Card 3–The strengths in the relationship

Here, the Devil shows that there is a physical attraction between the two people and that this is what is drawing them together.

Card 4–The obstacles in the relationship

The Star shows us that there are too many hopes and expectations placed on the relationship, either by Niamh or by her crush. This is frustrating for them both.

Card 5–Where you are right now

The Empress card usually indicates a feminine person who is happy in a relationship, so this card could mean that her crush has another love interest who is feeling more content.

Card 6–What influences are likely to come into play

An Ace of Cups can mean new beginnings. In this spread, it could indicate that Niamh's crush is more likely to have a new beginning with a different person.

Card 7–The outcome

The Two of Swords is a card of self-protection and fighting your corner. After her reading, Niamh can reflect on the messages that came up and then decide how to move forward in a positive way.

THE HORSESHOE SPREAD

For this spread, seven cards are laid out in a horseshoe shape. It can be helpful if you have a particular question to ask or if you just want a general reading.

Example: Jamie has asked for a general reading and has selected the seven cards shown.

The past–Three of Pentacles
The present–King of Swords
Hidden influences–The Empress
Obstacles that must be overcome–Six of Pentacles
Others' perspective–The Hermit
The best path to take–The Hierophant
The outcome–The Ace of Pentacles

EXPLANATION

Card 1–The past

The Three of Pentacles in the past position indicates that Jamie has been working hard to learn a skill of some kind. They have proven themselves and have been recognized for their achievements in some way.

Card 2–The present

The King of Swords here suggests that Jamie is in a strong position of authority right now. Perhaps their skills are being put to good use!

Card 3–Hidden influences

The Empress in this position means that a feminine figure has a hidden (and positive) influence over Jamie's life. It could be their mother or another person with similar energy.

Card 4–Obstacles that must be overcome

The Six of Pentacles indicates that Jamie wants to share their money or resources with others, but that this could be holding them back in some way. They may need to be careful or save for their future.

Card 5–Others' perspective

The Hermit suggests that others may be thinking that Jamie is difficult to reach. Jamie could be very busy and not have much time for loved ones right now.

Card 6–The best path to take

Here, the Hierophant suggests that Jamie needs to figure out what is most important, perhaps by seeking advice from someone older and wiser. Jamie has many questions about their purpose in life and may need to take time to gather their thoughts.

Card 7–The outcome

The Ace of Pentacles signifies that the outcome will be the start of a new venture. Jamie might say yes to a new opportunity. The high number of Major Arcana cards suggests that there is a higher purpose at work— Jamie's path will unfold as it should.

THE CELTIC CROSS SPREAD

The Celtic cross can offer great insight into a particular scenario or issue.

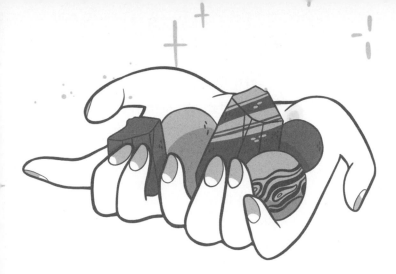

Example: Gabrielle has asked if she should buy her first car, but she is unsure if she should take on the responsibility.

A card to represent you–**The Devil**
The obstacle or influences that are impacting your question–
Two of Wands
The question itself–**Seven of Pentacles**
The recent past–**Ten of Pentacles**
The highest potential of the situation–**Page of Wands**
The near future–**Five of Cups**
Your fears and concerns–**Six of Wands**
Other people's perspectives–**The World**
Your hopes and wishes for the future–**The King of Wands**
The outcome–**Six of Pentacles**

EXPLANATION

Card 1–A card to represent you

The Devil card was randomly picked from the deck to represent Gabrielle. This doesn't mean that she is evil! It means that she needs to put her needs first in this matter.

Card 2–The obstacle or influences that are impacting your question

The Two of Wands here suggests that Gabrielle has put in a lot of effort to search for the right car, and now she has stopped to consider her options. Maybe she finds herself unable to close the deal.

Card 3–The question itself

The Seven of Pentacles has come up here. This reinforces the idea that Gabrielle is tired from her search. This tiredness could be what is keeping her from getting the car. She is advised to rest before making any moves.

Card 4–The recent past

The Ten of Pentacles in the recent past position suggests that Gabrielle has the money she needs to buy the car.

Card 5–The highest potential of the situation

The Page of Wands in this position represents a creative spirit being called to adventure! It suggests that she might not want to get tied down to one place right now.

Card 6–The near future

The Five of Cups here indicates that Gabrielle's dreams (of getting the car) may not come true. Maybe someone else will make a higher bid, or another situation will affect her decision.

Card 7–Your fears and concerns

The Six of Wands here suggests that Gabrielle is afraid of success. Everything she wants is in reach, but this may be causing anxiety to the point where she cannot act. She could spend some time reflecting on why she fears success—is she afraid of the responsibility that comes with it?

Card 8–Other people's perspectives

The World in this position indicates that other people think Gabrielle has the world at her feet! They may even be jealous—and this could be influencing her.

Card 9–Your hopes and wishes for the future

The King of Wands here suggests that Gabrielle has high aspirations. She dreams of journeying around the world before making any commitments. She should follow her intuition and take the path that allows her to realize her dreams.

Card 10–The overall outcome of the matter

The Six of Pentacles suggests that after achieving her dreams, Gabrielle will be able to share her success with others—she will find a way to use her resources for the benefit of all. Most of the cards in this reading are wands, followed by pentacles, which means that freedom and discovery take priority. After the situation predicted by card number 6 comes to pass, Gabrielle should be able to make decisions about the future.

The Major Arcana

The Fool

The Major Arcana starts with the Fool card and then witnesses the natural stages and trials that people experience as they grow up and mature or work to achieve their goals. The Fool's Journey is a symbolic journey through life.

"I SET OUT ON MY JOURNEY WITH TRUST AND A LIGHT HEART—THE WORLD OPENS UP FOR ME!"

Keywords: a fresh start, beginning, freedom, courage, openness, trust, risk-taking

The Fool is shown standing on the edge of a cliff, holding a travel bag in one hand and a rose in the other. He is stepping into the unknown and is alone except for his trusty dog. This card suggests that a new beginning is on the horizon and that courage will be needed to take the first step. The Fool is unaware of—and unprepared for—what awaits him, but through new experiences, he will begin to discover his potential.

The Magician

"I AM IN CHARGE OF MY DESTINY—I HOLD ALL THE KEYS TO MY SUCCESS!"

Keywords: skills, potential, mastery, resourcefulness, will, creativity, power, action

The Magician is standing next to a table, upon which there are items that represent each suit of the tarot. Some decks show him wearing a hat that is shaped like an infinity symbol, while others show the symbol floating above him. The Magician is holding his wand high up in the air to show that he is about to use his powers. At this first stage of his journey, the Fool realizes that he has everything he needs to succeed— he has become the Magician. He has the power to do good and overcome obstacles by being creative and resourceful.

The High Priestess

"I STAND BETWEEN WORLDS AND MANIFEST MY DESIRES."

Keywords: wisdom, intuition, mystery, secrets, hidden knowledge, unseen influences

The High Priestess is sitting between two pillars that mark the entrance to a sacred temple. She is holding a book of ancient knowledge on her lap. This figure stands for wisdom and intuition, and it represents the creative force of the feminine. When she appears in a reading, it could mean that there are hidden forces at work—and that we must look inward for an answer.

The Empress

"I AM LOVED AND CONTENT, FULLY ABLE TO GIVE AND RECEIVE LOVE."

Keywords: abundance, pleasure, contentment, creativity, nature, nurture, balance, fullness, aliveness, renewal

Seated on her throne, the Empress radiates a beauty that comes from her harmony with nature. She is the great Earth mother, in charge of the seasons, the fertility of the soil, and the production of the food that sustains us. At this stage of the journey, the Fool realizes that he needs to look after his health and physical needs. It can mean that with attention, a creative project will be successful—a situation is full of promise.

41

The Emperor

"I AM A RESPONSIBLE LEADER—I ALWAYS KNOW THE RIGHT ACTION TO TAKE."

Keywords: judgment, decision, action, responsibility, challenge, effectiveness, satisfaction from achievement

The Emperor is the card of fathering and indicates focus and the energy of accomplishment. The Emperor challenges the Fool to build something long-lasting that he can be proud of by deciding what he wants and values most in the world.

It will require hard work and determination for the Fool to achieve his goals, and his conduct will be judged. When this card is pulled, it can mean that someone in a position of authority is about to give important advice that should be taken seriously—and acted upon.

The Hierophant

"I AM WISDOM IN ALL ITS FORMS—
TAKE NOTICE OF ME AND YOU
SHALL THRIVE!"

Keywords: law, tradition, religion, meaning, philosophy, teaching, learning, vision

Also called the High Priest, the Hierophant is a wise teacher, priest, or counselor who can be relied upon during a time of crisis. At this stage in his journey, the Fool must seek answers to questions about the current purpose of his life. When this card appears in a spread, it indicates that we may be searching for meaning and need to approach the situation with a philosophical outlook.

The Lovers

"I WILL TAKE YOU TO THE PLACE WHERE DECISIONS MUST BE MADE."

Keywords: Love, connection, attraction, new possibilities, temptation, choice, union

This card shows a man and woman standing next to each other, with the man looking at the woman. The woman is looking up to the sky, where Cupid is watching, and on some decks, another person is standing next to them. The card speaks of love, relationship, and family, but it can also represent the need to make a choice. The card suggests that a union is possible, and there is hope for a bright future ahead if temptation can be avoided.

The Chariot

"I WILL GUIDE YOU TO YOUR GOAL."

Keywords: action, control, focus, strength, stability, willpower, conflict, struggle, change, triumph

The Chariot card shows the charioteer trying to control the two horses that are pulling the chariot. The horses represent two different principles pulling in opposite directions. The opposites that were united in the Lover card must now be kept moving in the same direction. At this stage in his journey, the Fool must use all his strength to keep on the right track. By seeing what must be done and taking control of the situation, obstacles will be overcome. If you manage to keep the opposing forces on the same path, you will go far!

Strength

Keywords: strength, control, confidence, balance, integrity, courage, generosity, compassion

The card of Strength shows a woman holding open (or forcing closed) the jaws of a lion, apparently without fear. The lion represents our primal urges—the wild animal within. Like the Magician, Strength has an infinity symbol above her head, indicating that she has achieved a new level of understanding. The Fool is gaining mastery over the forces that have governed him in the past, and he is taming his ego. This card suggests that struggles may be ahead, but that you have the courage and confidence to overcome any challenge.

The Hermit

"I WALK ALONE ON MY PATH TO FIND ENLIGHTENMENT."

Keywords: solitude, withdrawal, detachment, caution, patience, discretion, limitation

The Hermit stands alone on a mountaintop, holding up a lamp to light his way. He is wearing a cloak and carrying a staff to help him through the rough terrain. He has retreated from society to look inward for answers. Through patient searching, he has gained insight and has connected with his intuition. At this stage, the more mature Fool questions his direction in life. When this card appears in a spread, you may need to step away from a situation to recharge and think. You are advised to figure out what is important to you before taking any further action.

The Wheel of Fortune

"I AM ALWAYS TURNING—WHATEVER IS LOW WILL RISE AGAIN, AND WHATEVER IS HIGH WILL FALL."

Keywords: luck, chance, fortune, destiny, change, success, new direction

The Wheel of Fortune suggests that something unexpected is likely to happen and that it will change the outcome of an important matter. Although we are responsible for shaping our lives, it reminds us that luck and fortune can come along at any time. When the Wheel of Fortune is drawn, an unexpected solution to a problem may present itself. It may also predict opportunities and a new phase in life.

Justice

"I AM THE BALANCE THAT COMES WITH FAIR RECKONING ... "

Keywords: fairness, balance, reflection, decision, equality, truth, correct action

Justice is one of the underpinning principles of society. The figure on the card is pointing her sword upward, suggesting that justice will be upheld. The sword is double-edged, however; therefore, a balance must be found between two opposing forces for there to be a fair outcome. This is represented by the scales held in her other hand. Justice reminds us that we are accountable for our actions and urges us to always be honest and fair.

The Hanged Man

"I AM THE SACRIFICE WE MUST ALL MAKE TO FIND THE TRUTH."

Keywords: patience, waiting, surrender, sacrifice, wisdom, foresight, planning, strategy, eventual gain

This card shows a man hanging upside down from a beam. His legs are crossed, and his position shows that no progress is currently possible. The Hanged Man represents sacrifice and the willingness to face short-term losses to allow long-term gains. The Fool must learn patience and how to act strategically to achieve the result he wants. He may also benefit from a different perspective on the problems he is facing. This card can indicate that a current advantage must be given up, so that it can be replaced by a much better opportunity.

Death

"I AM THE CHANGE WE MUST ALL FACE TO BE REBORN ... "

Keywords: endings, loss, mourning, acceptance, adjustment, change, transition, rebirth, renewal

The card of Death shows a skeleton with a scythe. An era has ended, and a new one is about to begin. At this stage in the journey, the Fool must accept endings and uncertainty about the future. The endings may be very difficult and painful, but we must learn to accept them. After a period of mourning and adjustment, we will be able to move on and start on a new path. This card reminds us that change is inevitable and that as we gently come to terms with loss, we can enjoy a brighter future.

Temperance

"I AM THE KEY TO KEEPING YOUR HEAD."

Keywords: balanced tempers, harmony, moderation, cooperation, compromise, adaptability, relationship

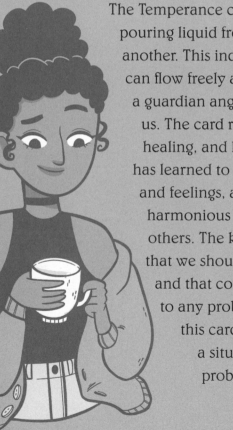

The Temperance card shows an angel pouring liquid from one vessel into another. This indicates that feelings can flow freely and can signify that a guardian angel is watching over us. The card represents balance, healing, and harmony. The Fool has learned to master his thoughts and feelings, and can now have harmonious relationships with others. The key message here is that we should act in moderation and that compromise is the key to any problem. When you pull this card, you can manage a situation and resolve problems. Success can be achieved!

The Devil

"I AM THE SHADOW YOU NEED TO SEE THE LIGHT."

Keywords: lust, greed, rage, primal instincts, secrets, the shadow, success in career, and personal interests

The Devil card asks us to confront the shadowy, instinctual part of ourselves. The Fool is reminded of the parts of himself that are self-serving and uncooperative, which he had tried to keep hidden away—even from himself. When this card appears in a spread, things that we don't like to admit about our character and desires may be trying to break into our awareness. We may experience these unwelcome qualities in others or in our dreams. A neglected

part of us needs to be heard. Personal gain and success in one's education or career are also indicated by this card. We are advised to act in our own best interests.

The Tower

"I AM THE CRISIS THAT IS THE MAKING OF YOU."

Keywords: conflict, overthrow, disruption, disapproval, sudden and unexpected change

The Tower card shows a tall building that has been struck by lightning. It is in flames and about to topple over. At this stage of his journey, the Fool encounters sudden, disruptive changes that force him to completely re-evaluate his path. This card suggests that times are volatile and that you may face uncertainty for awhile. If you pull this card in a reading, you shouldn't try to save whatever is toppling—it is better to stand back and wait for things to settle. A sudden, complete change may be the best way forward.

The Star

"I AM HOPE, BRIGHT AS THE STAR
NAMED SIRIUS … "

Keywords: hope, faith, meaning, inspiration, promise, healing, protection, new horizons

The Star is a welcome symbol of hope, inspiration, and rebirth to the Fool. In this card, we see a star shining brightly in the sky above a beautiful woman who is emptying pitchers of water into a stream. It represents feelings being returned to their source. Healing is possible, and our sense of well-being is renewed. There is hope for the future, and new possibilities are beginning to form. We are ready to give and receive love. The Star promises change for the better. This is a good time to meet new people, seek opportunities, and aspire toward what is important.

55

The Moon

"I AM THE FEAR THAT LURKS AT THE BOTTOM OF THE WATER."

Keywords: intuition, imagination, dreams, unconsciousness, fears, confusion, deception, disillusionment

The Moon is associated with night, the subconscious, and the dream world—where our deepest fears and imaginings run wild. The Fool has encountered a period of confusion and disillusionment. Where is the promise of the previous card, and what will happen next? If you pull this card, you are advised to be honest in your dealings with others and to steer away from paranoia. The way ahead is foggy, but you can trust your intuition to guide you.

The Sun

"I AM LIGHT AND WARMTH AND ALL
GOOD THINGS TO ALL PEOPLE."

Keywords: joy, optimism, clarity, trust, courage, ambition, success, opportunity, health, vitality, happiness

The Sun, shown shining on twin boys, is symbolic of life in full bloom! The Fool has passed through his dark night, and the way ahead is clear again. He knows where he is going and what he wants to achieve, and he is successful. Symbolizing energy, joy, optimism, and worldly success, this card suggests that it is the perfect moment to embrace opportunities and live life to the fullest. When this card appears in a spread, it promises good health and happiness!

57

Judgment

"I AM THE ONE WHO JUDGES THE WORTH
OF THOSE WHO COME BEFORE ME."

Keywords: reward for past effort, re-evaluation, responsibility, outcome,
resolution, acceptance

The Judgment card shows an angel playing the trumpet above figures rising from their graves. At this stage, the Fool is forced to review his choices so far. The card marks the point at which we must re-evaluate our lives. We may need to learn hard lessons or be held responsible for past actions—or we may be rewarded if we have acted with integrity. We are advised to seek solutions and move forward with a clean slate.

The World

"I COMPLETE THE CYCLE, SO THAT IT MAY TURN AGAIN AND BEGIN ANEW…"

Keywords: integration, contentment, achievement, completion, ending, final reward, success

The World, represented by a dancing woman, is the final card in one complete cycle. The Fool has accomplished much and learned what he is capable of along the way. Challenges have been faced and battles fought and won. He is now ready to take his position at the start of a new cycle. New challenges are calling, and they can be approached with confidence!

59

The Minor Arcana

Wands

Ace of Wands

Keywords: beginning, change, opportunity, adventure, creativity, hope, action

The Ace of Wands signifies new beginnings and opportunities! It suggests a chance to embark on a journey or an adventure—something that could significantly change the direction of a person's life. The situation is full of creative potential. If you pull this hopeful card, listen to your intuition, and say yes to new opportunities. Decide what you want to do and then act quickly!

Wands, shown as branches with sprouting leaves, are associated with the element of fire and represent the life force. There is a great deal of energy in the wands, which translates to action—sometimes creative and sometimes defensive or even aggressive. Many wands in a spread indicate that events are moving fast!

Two of Wands

Keywords: rest after hard work, patience, trust, planning

The Two of Wands indicates that a new goal or project is on the horizon. It has taken courage and determination to come up with your plan—now you can stand back and allow it to unfold. Leaving the matter alone to allow the magic to work can make you feel restless, but don't worry! Trust in the future. While you wait, make plans for the next stage of your life. What will you need to do once your goals have taken root and started to grow? This card suggests that negotiations may be needed, and that travel could be part of your journey.

Three of Wands

Keywords: accomplishment, success, satisfaction, progression

Congratulations, success is on the horizon! The Three of
Wands tells us that the first stage of a project has been
completed, and there is a great feeling of satisfaction and
pride. But remember—there is still a lot of work to do. Keep
working hard to continue the momentum you've gathered.
This will help you step into the next stage of your
project or goal.

Four of Wands

Keywords: reward, blessing, celebration, happiness, harmony, romance

The Four of Wands suggests that you can enjoy your success! It promises a restful time of peace and harmony before a storm. Soon, more hard work and energy will be needed to resolve any issues or conflicts that could come up. But for the time being, a celebration is in order! This card also serves as a reminder to share your success with others. Love could also be in the air!

Five of Wands

Keywords: fighting, conflict, obstacles, compromise

The fives of each tarot suit mark crunch points along the journey. The Five of Wands suggests conflict. In your effort to accomplish your goals, you may have had to make difficult decisions, perhaps stepping on people's toes along the way, or cutting corners. This may have been unavoidable, but now you must find a way to resolve the matter. If you behave with integrity, things can turn out to your advantage.

Six of Wands

Keywords: success, leadership, resolution, fortune

In the Six of Wands, problems have been dealt with and a matter is almost resolved. You have the support of your friends and family in achieving your goals. Good news is on the way, so it's important that you don't give up now. Stay true to your original vision. This card may indicate that you will receive praise for your efforts. If you have exams, the results are likely to be positive. Relationships are about to take a turn for the better. What a great card!

Seven of Wands

Keywords: upper hand, the position of advantage, challenge, force, reassessment

With the Seven of Wands, you face another challenge with others, but this time you have the upper hand. If you remember to play fair as you apply force, you'll harness your competitive nature. The challenges you face will also help you reassess your plans and goals, so that you can make any necessary changes. This will make you stronger and more successful in the long run.

Eight of Wands

Keywords: movement, progress, back on track, goals on their way to being achieved

The Eight of Wands represents a plan on its way to completion. You are back on track after a time of conflict and delay. Obstacles have been cleared and the way is free, which means you can forge ahead with your plans—things are on the move! This card also means that events are changing quickly and that soon circumstances will change for the better. Things you have hoped for will come to pass. Travel may be needed to complete a task.

Nine of Wands

Keywords: final challenge, the goal in sight, perseverance, tenacity, determination, courage to overcome.

The Nine of Wands represents last-minute challenges on your way to attaining a goal. You have come a long way and are determined not to give up now! Although it may not seem like it, what you have been hoping for is in reach. With your goal in sight, you find the courage to make one final push. If you persevere, nothing can stand in your way for long. You must find the resources to keep going from deep within. Remain hopeful—you have been given a chance to prove that you are worthy of success, and now it is up to you to rise to the challenge.

Ten of Wands

Keywords: achievement, attainment of goals, satisfaction, experience gained, rest and regeneration are needed

In the Rider-Waite-Smith deck, the Ten of Wands shows an old man reaching his destination. He is hunched over with the weight of his load. You have come a long way and are weighed down with the responsibility of turning your vision into reality. Your efforts will pay off, but there has been the loss of youthful innocence and optimism along the way. You can find satisfaction in your achievements, but remember to rest and recharge, so that you can start the creative process again.

Page of Wands

Keywords: active, playful, imaginative, inspired, creative, youthful foolishness

The Page of Wands is boisterous with an active imagination! This card represents the urge to explore and play, follow your dreams, and look for new experiences. The Page seeks to avoid the responsibility that comes with maturity. When it appears in a reading, it may represent a person (of any age) whose actions are always youthful. It could also mean that you need to break from habits that no longer serve you, so that you can develop these creative qualities in yourself.

Knight of Wands

Keywords: noble, courageous, hasty, unreliable, aggressive, volatile, new direction

The Knight of Wands is a great warrior. He loves to take risks and prove that he is worthy. He defends the vulnerable and fights for their cause, and he can be hot-headed. The card may describe someone you know, or it could indicate that you need to develop some warrior-like qualities. The Knight of Wands also often signifies a move to a new home or a new direction in life.

Queen of Wands

Keywords: strong, courageous, generous, vibrant, creative, wise, intuitive

The Queen of Wands is a wise woman. She's independent, authoritative, imaginative, intuitive, strong, and courageous! Essentially, she knows what she wants and how to get it. The queen makes a warm, lively, and generous host. The card may describe a woman with these characteristics—or it may suggest that it is time for you to develop these qualities for yourself.

King of Wands

Keywords: intuitive, decisive, active, inspirational, visionary

The King of Wands is a mature man of vision who inspires others. He has strong leadership qualities and uses his wisdom and powers of intuition to guide his decision-making. He is also sprightly and full of energy—this king enjoys living life to the fullest! This card could describe someone you know that is like this, or it could mean that it is time for you to develop the qualities of leadership, activity, and inspiration yourself.

Ace of Cups

Keywords: love, joy, happiness, abundance, relationship, emotional expression, fertility

The Ace of Cups, like the overflowing waters pictured on some card decks, indicates free-flowing emotions that need to be expressed. When this card comes up there is potential for great emotional contentment—deeply satisfying love and happiness are possible. The Ace of Cups represents the start of a new relationship. There is a chance for a fresh start and a new lease of life. There is great hope for the future—your emotions will sustain you, and love will find a way!

Cups are associated with the element of water. They represent feelings, love, relationships, and emotional contentment because water quenches our thirst and brings satisfaction. Cups also represent the imagination and subconscious. The cups themselves are vessels for holding water and are often shown full; however, sometimes the water is spilled (indicating crisis and sorrow) or overflowing (suggesting abundance). Many cups in a spread show that feelings and relationships are highlighted.

Two of Cups

Keywords: a new relationship, attraction, romance, harmony, satisfaction, conception, emotional contentment

The Two of Cups is a sign of the start of a new relationship or connection with another person. This new development has the capacity for deep satisfaction and contentment—it feels as though you have met your match. You see yourself reflected in this person and find new aspects of yourself through their eyes. Existing relationships are strengthened. This card can also indicate marriage, a baby, or another creative endeavor.

Three of Cups

Keywords: pleasure, joy, marriage, birth, feasting, merriment, celebration, abundance, fortune

The Three of Cups indicates that there will be a happy gathering of people. It may bring news of a pregnancy, marriage proposal, or success in a creative endeavor close to your heart. You can be proud of your achievements—joy and cause for celebration are indicated. This is a time to share your good fortune with others. You have renewed faith in the power of love!

Four of Cups

Keywords: dissatisfaction, boredom, discontent, depression, crisis, re-evaluation, self-questioning

This card indicates that you are unhappy and in danger of developing a careless attitude toward life. You may be entering a period of questioning everything and could have lost touch with your loved ones. You may also feel that something is lost or missing from your life and can't see how lucky you are. Take some time to re-evaluate your life and decide what truly matters to you.

Five of Cups

Keywords: loss, sorrow, regret, despair, betrayal, neglect, emotional breakdown, relationship breakup

The Five of Cups can signal a relationship breakdown. The image on some decks shows a man in a black cloak turning his back and withdrawing from the world. Three cups have been spilled on the ground, indicating that relationships have been lost or thrown away. Importantly, however, two full cups remain—this means that you have a chance to hold on to what is left. Think carefully before coming to a decision.

Six of Cups

Keywords: calm, serenity, acceptance, simple pleasures, nostalgia, old friends, hope and opportunity

The Six of Cups is the calm after an emotional storm. Although things might not be perfect, you can learn to accept your limits and find a new appreciation for those close to you. Your thoughts may be overly focused on the past if you pull this card. An old friend may re-enter your life and help you come to terms with who you now are, bringing a fresh opportunity and a new lease on life. New friendships can also blossom.

Seven of Cups

Keywords: decision, choice, dream, vision, imagination, a new path

The Seven of Cups suggests that you are at a crossroads in your life or a particular matter. You have an important decision to make, and there appears to be more than one choice. Each cup in this card is filled with a different option. You may rely on the imagination, a dream, or a vision to choose the right path, but you are advised to remain grounded and realistic when working with the imaginary realm or your decisions will be short-lived. Think before you choose.

Eight of Cups

Keywords: retreat, escape, abandonment, loss, dissatisfaction, time out, perspective needed

The Eight of Cups indicates that you may need some space to figure out what is important to you. You feel unfulfilled and dissatisfied with your choices, and are finding it difficult to choose something and stick with it. To move forward, you must find a way to gain some perspective on your life. You may also need to lose something for awhile before it comes back.

Nine of Cups

Keywords: wishes fulfilled, hopes realized, positive outcome, birth, joy, success, reward

The Nine of Cups is known as the nine months card because it can indicate the birth of a baby or the completion of a creative project. You are brimming with joy, and the world is filled with hope again! Health and happiness are here, and the problems of the past have passed. A wish will be fulfilled, and things will work out unexpectedly well.
Enjoy your good fortune!

Ten of Cups

Keyword: lasting happiness, joy, contentment, emotional stability, a fortunate outcome

The Ten of Cups is a card of emotional security and long-lasting fortune in love. More happiness than you might have thought possible will be yours. A stable, lasting relationship and future family life are indicated. You can relax and enjoy the rewards of your efforts and good fortune—a situation has the best outcome.

Page of Cups

Keywords: sensitive, sympathetic, kind, imaginative, poetic, lazy, daydreamer

The Page of Cups is a sensitive young soul—a kind, generous person who is easily hurt, feels people's pain, and is sympathetic to their needs. The Page may be naturally lazy at times and is prone to daydreaming. He needs plenty of space to play and explore his imagination. This card could refer to someone with these qualities, or it may indicate that these characteristics need to be developed in yourself. This card can also indicate that news from a loved one may be on its way.

Knight of Cups

Keywords: romantic, chivalrous, idealistic, questing, highly principled, on a mission

The Knight of Cups rides around the kingdom searching for his love, ready to save her from any misfortune and then ride off into the sunset! The Knight may also be on another quest—to see the Holy Grail and restore the health of the King, bringing balance, peace, and harmony to the kingdom. This card may describe someone in your life who has a sense of mission and high ideals, or it can refer to these qualities in your character.

Queen of Cups

Keyword: emotional, sensitive, caring, peace-loving, harmonious, imaginative, creative talents

The Queen of Cups is in touch with her feelings. Wise and peace-loving, she is in tune with others. She is sensitive, sympathetic, and kind-hearted. A good listener, she can give good advice. The queen is a highly imaginative woman with creative gifts and talents. This card can represent a mature woman within your life, or it can refer to these qualities in your character.

King of Cups

Keywords: kind, honest, responsible, respected, considerate, easily swayed

The King of Cups is a kind and noble figure who is trusted and respected by others. He is naturally caring and puts the needs of others first. He has a position of power and is a fair ruler. Because of this, he has earned the respect of others. The negative side of this character is that he can be manipulated, which means he can become distrustful of others' motives. This card can represent a figure in your life with these qualities, or it can refer to these qualities in your character.

Ace of Swords

Keywords: beginning, hope, ideals, principles, justice, new direction

The Ace of Swords stands for your principles and ideals. You have decided to start something new and have high expectations of your future. Justice will be done. You do not wish to compromise your strongly held beliefs. You are asked to have faith in yourself and your ability to overcome any challenges that lie ahead.

Swords are associated with the element of air and represent ideas, rational thought, and justice. The sword cards describe circumstances that require you to fight for your beliefs. Their blades are double-edged, indicating that every decision you make may have both beneficial and harmful consequences. Swords are made of cold, hard metal, suggesting a lack of feeling or emotion. Several swords in a spread indicate a focus on thinking—you may be called to fight or forced to reconsider your beliefs and ideals.

Two of Swords

Keywords: tension, balance, difficult decision, action needed

The Two of Swords indicates that something is hanging in the balance, and a difficult decision must be made. You cannot decide what to do, but you must make a decision and stick with it! You should act now and not allow fears and doubts to hold you back. The sooner you decide, the sooner you can move on and find relief.

Three of Swords

Keywords: conflict, struggle, heartache, disappointment, arguments, fears, separation

The Three of Swords suggests pain and disappointment in matters of the heart—arguments with loved ones are indicated, and separation of some kind may be the result. Some distance will help you find relief, however, and once you have tended to your grief, you will see that change was necessary for the future.

Four of Swords

Keywords: rest, retreat, withdrawal, recuperation, relief from anxieties, rebuilding strength

The Four of Swords shows that something has been lost and part of you feels as though it has died with it. You need time alone to reflect on what has happened and how things might have gone wrong. Now, you must rebuild your strength and reorganize your thoughts before you are ready to face the world again.

Five of Swords

Keywords: unfair play, unethical, loss, facing consequences

The Five of Swords indicates acting without consideration of the consequences. You may have acted in an unethical way to gain the upper hand in a matter, but now your victory is causing you sorrow. To move forward, you must approach the situation honestly and be prepared to face the music.

Six of Swords

Keywords: solace, respite, retreat, healing, journey, insight, reputation restored

The Six of Swords suggests that your strength has been sapped by a particularly tough time, but thankfully the worst has now passed. It indicates that a journey may be the best way to resolve a matter. This may be an internal journey of the mind, or you may travel somewhere. Either way, you are being confronted by subconscious thoughts, and as a result, insights may arise. To find a resolution, allow things to resolve on their own without intervening.

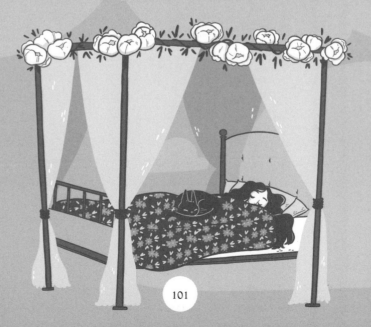

Seven of Swords

Keywords: cunning, guile, deceit, tact, diplomacy, flexibility, compromise for the greater good

In some decks, the Seven of Swords shows a figure stealing swords from a military camp. This represents taking an action that may be necessary for the greater good, even if it means going against your principles. The card suggests that there are times when your beliefs and ideals must be flexible and should adapt to the task at hand. This is because life throws many situations at us, and we can't afford to be too rigid in our thinking to deal with them.

Eight of Swords

Keywords: restriction, mistrust, inability to act, indecision, imprisonment, isolation from others

The Eight of Swords represents restriction and mistrust. A situation seems hopeless, and you can't see a way out. You may feel trapped and hemmed in by your insistence on going it alone. You have run out of excuses and ways to avoid making a decision— there is no escape. You must learn to trust people and ask for help. You need to rebuild your connection with others and end your isolation before a decision is possible.

Nine of Swords

Keywords: fear, doubt, anxiety, nightmares, troubled conscience, suffering, despair

The Nine of Swords represents anxiety and suffering. It suggests that your hopes have been dashed and that you are filled with fear and doubt. You are likely blaming yourself for an unfortunate outcome, but you need to keep things in perspective. While it is necessary to own your part in a situation, you are only human and will make mistakes. You need to forgive and accept yourself before you can move on.

Ten of Swords

Keywords: endings, misfortune, loss, defeat, new understanding, fresh perspective

The Ten of Swords represents defeat and marks the end of a difficult situation. At the end of the long struggle, something has been lost. Ultimately, the outcome isn't what you wanted, but you must put the past behind you that so you can move forward. While you have been defeated this time, you have also learned important lessons that can give you a fresh perspective on life—and yourself.

Page of Swords

Keywords: curiosity, intelligence, wit, honesty, independence, clash with authority

The Page of Swords is a clever, witty youth with a natural curiosity and inquisitive nature! He is in the process of developing his ideas and beliefs, and he may frequently clash with authority. His ideas and curious spirit should be encouraged and nurtured rather than squashed. This card can represent a person who displays these qualities, or it may suggest that the person being read for needs to develop these characteristics.

Knight of Swords

Keywords: fighter, warrior, reformer, prepared to make sacrifices for just causes

The Knight of Swords is a brave warrior who fights for the causes he believes in. The knight challenges injustice wherever he sees it and shows courage against all odds. He is willing to make sacrifices to uphold his principles and fights for justice, fairness, and reform. The change will be brought about. This card can represent a person who displays these qualities, or it may suggest that the person being read for needs to develop these characteristics.

Queen of Swords

Keywords: just, fair, intelligent, faithful, warrior, strong beliefs, idealistic, highly principled

The Queen of Swords has a strong mind and is intelligent. She may seem icy or aloof, but she is always kind and fair toward her people. This Queen will argue her opinions with a clear head, and she is not afraid to fight for her principles if necessary. When this card is selected, it may represent someone who displays these qualities, or it could suggest that they need to be developed.

King of Swords

The King of Swords is intelligent and known for his clear head and sense of logic. He is an excellent judge and counselor to his people, as well as a capable warrior and military strategist. He has many innovative ideas. He encourages reform and change, and runs an orderly, civilized society. When this card is selected, it may represent someone who displays these qualities, or it could suggest that they need to be developed.

Pentacles

Ace of Pentacles

Keywords: new venture, opportunity, the promise of wealth, achievement

The Ace of Pentacles suggests a new opportunity or venture that will put our talents to good use. Like the other aces, this card represents high hopes for success and an opportunity to make something of our talents, provided that we use them wisely. If you are experiencing scarcity in your life, it can predict that a period of abundance is on the way.

Pentacles are associated with the element of earth and represent matter, the body, and the physical world. They are concerned with financial security, as well as personal values and the security that comes from within. This suit represents physical health and well-being and the ability to take comfort from personal possessions and the physical world. The pentacles are in the shape of coins, suggesting money. The pentacles can also represent talents and abilities that might help us earn money and contribute to society in a useful way. Many pentacles in a spread suggest that material gain is highlighted, and that action may be required.

Two of Pentacles

Keywords: balance, weighing up pros and cons, careful
consideration, common sense, responsible decision-making

The Two of Pentacles is concerned with juggling
two different duties, weighing up the pros and cons
of a situation, and making a carefully considered
decision. In the image on the Rider-Waite-Smith deck,
the figure balances two pentacles that are connected
by the infinity symbol. This indicates that the figure
must keep all their responsibilities in balance. If you
pull this card, you are being challenged to make the
most practical choice you can.

Three of Pentacles

Keywords: craftsperson, skilled artisan, recognition of abilities, achievement

The Three of Pentacles indicates that you will be recognized for your skills and achievements. You have worked hard to earn your success so far, and this has been noticed. While establishing a new venture, you have honed your skills and built a good reputation. Now you must reassess your goals and develop a new direction. Your next project can start from a position of strength.

Four of Pentacles

Keywords: thrift, overprotectiveness, lack of generosity, mistrust, paranoia, isolation

The Four of Pentacles represents a withholding, ungenerous nature. You are afraid of losing what you've got, so you hold on tightly to everything and feel paranoid about other people's motives. This card can show that you are so afraid of losing what you have that you lose touch with others and become unapproachable. It can indicate a fear of taking risks, a fear of illness, or obsessions. It warns that self-imposed isolation and a need for control mean you could push away those who love you.

Five of Pentacles

Keywords: financial worries, fear of loss, destitution, failure, shame, re-evaluation, starting again

The Five of Pentacles indicates financial worries and a fear of loss or failure. It suggests both material and spiritual lack and may be predicting the failure of a venture. It can show that you have not lived up to your high standards and expectations. Importantly, it may have been your fear of loss that has led to this situation. You must reassess your actions and regain faith in your talents. You can work hard, rebuild your reputation, and achieve your ambitions.

Six of Pentacles

Keywords: success, sharing of wealth, charity, philanthropy, giving back to society

The Six of Pentacles signifies the sharing of good fortune with others. You have learned the lesson of the previous cards and now understand the consequences of holding on too tightly to material possessions. Plans are working out; you have succeeded in rebuilding your reputation and can celebrate your success with others. Satisfaction is gained from sharing time and money with worthy causes.

Seven of Pentacles

Keywords: rest after work, disappointing returns, re-evaluation of projects, redirecting efforts

The Seven of Pentacles indicates weariness after a period of hard work and suggests pausing to assess what you have achieved so far. It asks you to re-evaluate your plans and take stock of a situation. Are you on the best route to success? Perhaps you are overworked and disappointed with the rewards of your hard work. A period of rest may be necessary, and you might want to take a short break if you can. Keep the faith while implementing improvements.

Eight of Pentacles

Keywords: new skills, apprenticeship, confidence, job satisfaction, rewards

The Eight of Pentacles represents learning a new skill. You are slowly but surely gaining mastery and can reap the rewards of your efforts so far. Financial gain is indicated, so have faith in your skills and be confident in your ability to achieve your ambitions. Stay on the path!

Nine of Pentacles

Keywords: pleasure, self-esteem, humility, realistic evaluation, sense of achievement, satisfaction, windfall

The Nine of Pentacles indicates that you can take pleasure and satisfaction in your work and reap the rewards. You have worked hard to develop your talents and abilities, and you have proved yourself a capable and worthy member of your community. You are realistic about your limitations and recognize that you have had failures along the way. However, you can be proud of everything you have achieved so far and can draw satisfaction from recognizing your journey to success. An unexpected windfall is also indicated!

Ten of Pentacles

Keywords: security, inheritance, lasting success, satisfaction, sharing, rewards, contentment

Congratulations! The Ten of Pentacles indicates success has been achieved! You have earned the right to relax and enjoy whatever has been gained by your efforts. This card suggests that you have also developed an inner sense of security. This card can also suggest that you may come into an inheritance. Enjoying the company of your family and loved ones and sharing your wealth with them brings you great pleasure. This card indicates a happy home life.

Page of Pentacles

Keywords: diligent, reliable, mature, loyal, steady, hard-working, responsible

The Page of Pentacles is mature beyond their years and is the type of youth you can depend on—reliable, hard-working, and enthusiastic about work. He makes a loyal, steady friend. The Page represents a youthful person who displays these qualities, or it can highlight the need to nurture these qualities in ourselves. This card can mean that a message about money is on its way.

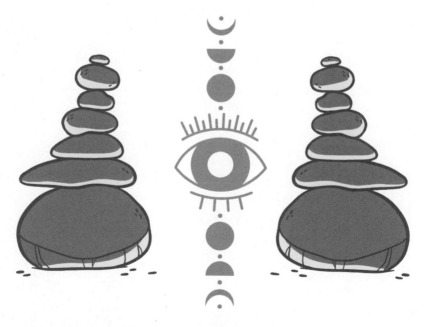

Knight of Pentacles

Keywords: sensible, considerate, stable, responsible, respectful, practical, nervous

The Knight of Pentacles is a practical, sensible, considerate character, with a strong sense of duty and respect for others. Unlike the other knights, the Knight of Pentacles acts with caution to avoid rocking the boat. Knights are normally very active, fighting for a change of some kind. This knight needs to find a way of balancing these two tendencies, or he will be pulled in different directions. This card can represent a person with these qualities, or it can indicate the need to develop them in ourselves.

Queen of Pentacles

Keywords: generous, stable, sensible, down-to-earth, warm, comforting, healthy, contented

The Queen of Pentacles is practical, down-to-earth, and generous. She has an affinity with nature and animals and radiates comfort and confidence in her body. She enjoys taking care of others and tending to her surroundings. This queen can be relied upon to give fair, sensible advice and find practical solutions to problems. The card can represent a mature person who displays these qualities, or it can highlight the need to develop them in ourselves.

King of Pentacles

Keywords: sensible, fair, honest, patient, generous, practical, traditional, stable, humble, self-reliant

The King of Pentacles is an honest, generous leader who has worked hard and has achieved great success! He upholds his duties and traditions, and he respects his ancestral heritage. The king finds practical solutions to problems and dislikes new methods or technologies. This king is kind, but he has high expectations of others and expects them to have the same self-discipline and work ethic that he has. He is humble and self-reliant. This card can represent a mature man who displays these qualities, or it can indicate the need to develop them in ourselves.

Index

THE WORLD IS FULL OF MAGICAL THINGS, PATIENTLY WAITING FOR OUR SENSES TO GROW SHARPER.

W.B. YEATS

Other titles in the series:
Spells * Crystals * Astrology * Palm Reading *
Divination * Manifesting * Spells and Charms